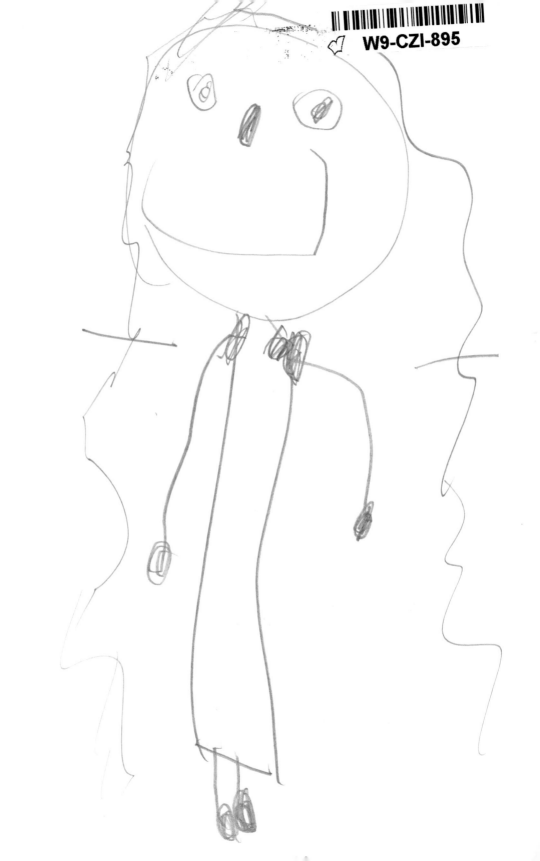

TOOLS FOR CAREGIVERS

- **F&P LEVEL:** C
- **WORD COUNT:** 33
- **CURRICULUM CONNECTIONS:** holidays, traditions

Skills to Teach

- **HIGH-FREQUENCY WORDS:** a, get, I, is, it, see, today, we
- **CONTENT WORDS:** bats, black, carved, cats, costumes, fun, Halloween, holiday, orange, pumpkins, spooky, treats, trick-or-treat, wear
- **PUNCTUATION:** exclamation points, periods
- **WORD STUDY:** /k/, spelled c (*costumes*); /k/, spelled *ck* (*black, trick*); long /a/, spelled *ay* (*holiday, today*); long /e/, spelled *ea* (*treats*); long /e/, spelled *ee* (*Halloween, see*); multisyllable word (*Halloween*); /oo/, spelled *oo* (*spooky*)
- **TEXT TYPE:** factual description

Before Reading Activities

- Read the title and give a simple statement of the main idea.
- Have students "walk" through the book and talk about what they see in the pictures.
- Introduce new vocabulary by having students predict the first letter and locate the word in the text.
- Discuss any unfamiliar concepts that are in the text.

After Reading Activities

Flip back through the book as a group. Pages 6 and 7 talk about costumes. What costumes are the children wearing on these pages? What other costumes do readers see in the book? Have the readers ever dressed up for Halloween? What were they? What would they like to dress up as?

Tadpole Books are published by Jump!, 5357 Penn Avenue South, Minneapolis, MN 55419, www.jumplibrary.com

Copyright ©2022 Jump! International copyright reserved in all countries. No part of this book may be reproduced in any form without written permission from the publisher.

Editor: Jenna Gleisner **Designer:** Molly Ballanger

Photo Credits: Shutterstock, cover, 2tl, 2mr, 4–5; Benjamin Simeneta/Shutterstock, 1; Chih Yuan Wu/Dreamstime, 3; all_about_people/ Shutterstock, 2ml, 6; Ebtikar/Shutterstock, 7; kali9/iStock, 2br, 8–9; 5 second Studio/Shutterstock, 2bl, 10–11; Hollygraphic/Shutterstock, 2tr, 12–13; adriaticfoto/Shutterstock, 14–15; Joshua Resnick/Shutterstock, 16.

Library of Congress Cataloging-in-Publication Data
Names: Zimmerman, Adeline J., author.
Title: Halloween / by Adeline J. Zimmerman.
Description: Minneapolis: Jump!, Inc., 2022. | Series: Holiday fun! | Includes index. | Audience: Ages 3–6
Identifiers: LCCN 2020047190 (print) | LCCN 2020047191 (ebook) | ISBN 9781636900872 (hardcover)
ISBN 9781636900889 (paperback) | ISBN 9781636900896 (ebook)
Subjects: LCSH: Halloween—Juvenile literature.
Classification: LCC GT4965 .Z56 2022 (print) | LCC GT4965 (ebook) | DDC 394.2646—dc23
LC record available at https://lccn.loc.gov/2020047190
LC ebook record available at https://lccn.loc.gov/2020047191

HALLOWEEN

by Adeline J. Zimmerman

TABLE OF CONTENTS

tadpole
books

WORDS TO KNOW

bats

carved

costumes

pumpkins

treats

trick-or-treat

HALLOWEEN

Today is Halloween!

bat

I see black bats.

pumpkin

I see orange pumpkins.

We wear costumes.

We trick-or-treat.

We get treats.

treats

Fun!

We see carved pumpkins.

Spooky!

It is a fun holiday!

LET'S REVIEW!

A holiday is a special day. Halloween is on October 31. How is this family celebrating?

INDEX